My New Sister

Rebecca Hunter

Photography by Chris Fairclough

Evans

First published in this edition in 2009 by Evans Brothers Ltd
2A Portman Mansions
Chiltern Street
London WIU 6NR
England

Reprinted 2010

Hunter, Rebecca
My new sister, - (First Time)
1. Sister - Juvenile literature 2. Infants (Newborn)
1. Title
306.8'75

ISBN 978 0 237 53857 6

Acknowledgements
Planning and production by Discovery Books
Editor: Rebecca Hunter
Photographer: Chris Fairclough
Designer: Ian Winton
© Evans Brothers Limited 2000

Consultant: Trevor Jellis M.A., M.Phil., A.F.B.Ps., Psychol. is a Chartered Psychologist who
has spent thirty years working with individuals, schools, companies and major corporate
institutions in the management of stress. He deals with individuals who are suffering from
stress both in their family life and in the workplace.

The publishers would like to thank Bethan and Angharad Evans, Jackie and
Peter Evans, Megan and Lisa Davies and the Knighton Hospital
for their help in the preparation of this book.

My New Sister

**My name is Bethan.
This book tells you about
my new baby sister.**

Contents

Mum is going to have a baby.

Mum is going to have a baby soon. She lets me feel the baby kicking in her tummy.

Mum is tired.

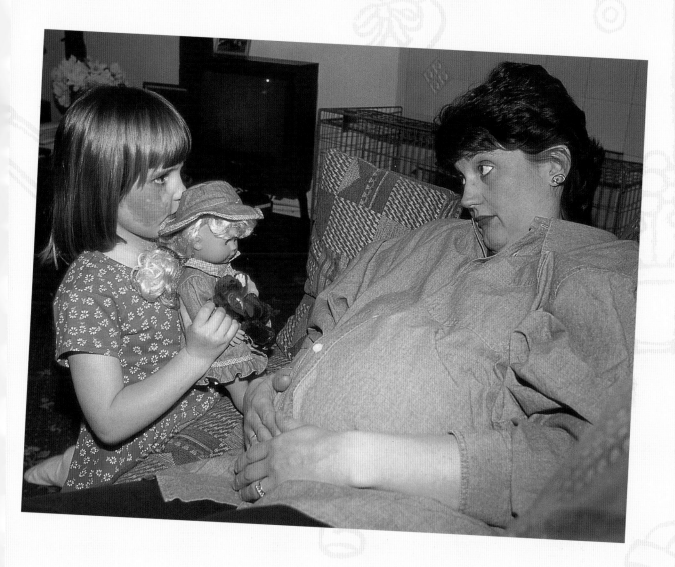

Mum is often tired and can't always play with me.

We are getting ready.

Dad and I are getting out the baby things.

The baby has lots of tiny clothes. I like these little boots best.

Everyone is busy.

Everyone is busy getting things ready. I hope they will still have time for me.

Mum has gone to the hospital.

Mum has gone to the hospital to have the baby. I am spending the day with my Grandma.

I am drawing a picture.

I am drawing a picture
for the baby.

Grandma is helping me.

I have a new baby sister.

Mum has had the baby.
I have a new baby sister.

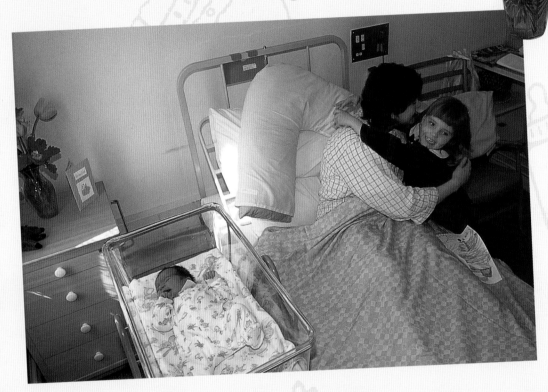

Dad and I go to see Mum and the
baby in the hospital. I am very
glad to see Mum again.

She is very small.

My new baby sister's name is Megan.

She is very small but Mum lets me hold her. She doesn't look at my picture at all.

My baby sister cries a lot.

My baby sister sleeps a lot and cries a lot. She is too young to play with.

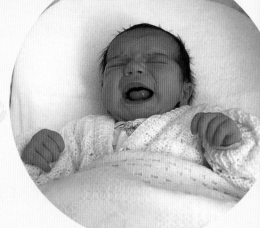

I don't like my baby sister very much.

I get cross and shout at her. Now Mum is cross with me. I don't like my baby sister very much.

Dad and I are looking after Megan.

Dad and I are looking after Megan today. She is eight weeks old now and smiles at me.

I show him what to do.

Dad is not very good
at changing nappies.
I show him what to do.

My baby sister is growing up.

Megan is nine months old now. She likes to play with me and I read her stories.

I love my
baby sister.

I love my baby sister. When she
is bigger we will have lots of fun.

Index

Notes to Parents

It is hard to exaggerate the level of stress that a child will experience when they realise that another member of the family is about to be born. During the mother's pregnancy, the child will feel resentful at all the new things that are bought and the excitement that everyone feels for a person who does not yet exist. Once the baby is born, the limelight passes from the child to the new arrival, and the child, (particularly if an only child), may feel completely unloved and ignored. Many children revert to babyish speech and behaviour as a way of seeking attention.

Preparing children well in advance is absolutely vital. From the age of two or three, the possibility of the child having brothers and sisters can be talked about. The child should not actually be told about the expected baby until a few months before the birth. Nine months is a very long time for a small child to wait. At this stage all the positive aspects of a sibling can be emphasised. The child can help the parents prepare a room for the baby and their opinion can be sought on what colour clothes or choice of equipment should be bought. All children should enjoy the thought of having someone new to play with.

Mum's departure to hospital should be discussed well beforehand. The child should know who will look after them when this happens and that Dad will come and tell them the news first of all. When Mum returns home with the new baby the child should be encouraged to look upon themselves as an important helper and made to feel that their contribution to helping Mum and Dad with the baby is very important.

• When buying things for the new baby, the child should also be included with little presents.

• Friends, grandparents and other members of the family should be encouraged to give the child as much attention as the new baby.